C000261425

THE GOLDFISH

ABOUT THE AUTHOR

Ikhda Ayuning Maharsi Degoul is an Indonesian poet currently based in Japan. Her debut pamphlet, *Ikhda by Ikhda*, was published by the Emma Press in 2014. Her poems have been published in *The Emma Press Anthology of Mildly Erotic Verse* and *The Emma Press Anthology of Motherhood.*

ABOUT THE ILLUSTRATOR

Emma Dai'an Wright is a British-Chinese-Vietnamese publisher and illustrator based in Birmingham. She studied Classics at Brasenose College, Oxford, and worked in ebook production at Orion Publishing Group before leaving in 2012 to set up the Emma Press.

AUTHOR'S NOTE— *The Goldfish* is a collection of provocations and statements on feminism. I tried to challenge myself to play with dualities and intensely compare the lives of a woman and a goldfish in a glass bowl. The spontaneous, surreal and playful words are an energetic encouragement to all individuals living and thinking in the new world. The world of cross-cultural thought and divergence.

THE EMMA PRESS

First published in the UK in 2019 by the Emma Press Ltd

ISBN 978-1-912915-20-0

A CIP catalogue record of this book is available from the British Library.

Printed and bound in Great Britain by Oxuniprint Ltd, Oxford.

The Emma Press
theemmapress.com
hello@theemmapress.com
Birmingham, UK

POEMS BY IKHDA AYUNING MAHARSI DEGOUL

ILLUSTRATED BY EMMA DAI'AN WRIGHT

I SWIM TO FIND
MY SELF;
I SWIM AND
I BREATHE

THE GOLDFISH

Stars are starving

Cats are getting mad

My mouth
wide open

O what I—

I need to be a newborn
immediately
delivered by a long river

O what I—
I
need
to give birth to the newest me every day

Ovulating my apperception

Bursting splashing sparkling!

Blubbbb blubb blub blu bl b bbbeat about the bbbbushhhh (gasp)

The short high voltage memory inside my head is not even pardonable

Stimulations everywhere Suddenly I get stoned Abruptly I forget everything

Paradoxical silly
I just can't keep all of it inside my whimsical belly
I forget all things All the time

O memory Anamnesis Trophy

(gasp)

I am inhuman
I am a flower who moves I am red
A bundle of nerves

Stop and go
This space contains my constant chagrin

Too many crashed stones
Capricious environs
I need oxygen

Outbreak!
For that I bathe

Up up up!
Exhalation
Inhalation
Habouh habouh haboubouh habouh

Inhibition
O next scale of life O *l'évolution!*

Fine!

It's time to be severe
Terre sucks, I would rather be in water

A covalent molecule
Two atoms
Hydrogen
and oxygen

O self phenomenon

I am inhuman
A cheerful fish with superb disease

A blank

Dancing flower

Lapse of memory Entertainment for humans

The old hypocrisy:

Sad dude It's sad yes

Rigidity doesn't work

in the world of fishesesesessesssssssssssss

My world

Sunset is here

All the fish are getting into the tunes The tunes of the water

The water surrounding the continent The continent of the universe

The universe is a fantasiser

daydreamer

Happy ending swan song

TO THE GENTLE RIVER

Sleepless on the river

Listen to the bubbling water   Serene at a standstill

It is time to study

Hush   human   hush

How is it correct to say that
everything beyond the water has its bogus   artificial
apocryphal   sham   spurious   dummy
instruments

How is it correct to give persistence and resistance to the counterfeit endeavours of human beings

Goodness of my red colour   turning into gold

I can even remember some of their gibberish
Hhhhhhhhhhhhhhhhhhh human
Buff! Bouf! Boo! Plouf!
Pop off!

Thank you for those, you average, widespread, popular westbound

I swim more kilometres in Kamogawa
looking for the delicious *nori* to show me
the glory of my plainness is sincere

REBELLION RED

The clown is here
regarding all the instruments on the bar

Regarding all the liquors
Being banned
Being cursed to live forever inside the glass pool

Installed in the small aquarium
while the mooniest drinker continues observing me
with his desperate gasping

He never stops burping

Grumbling

Swearing at the system

Cursing the existence
of positivity

So man-ish So chestnut So blah blah

O revolt!

Rebellion red!

I refuse to be a clown anymore

I dislike those yucky tidbits
and I am going to jump for real

I am not a de-stresser   for anyone

Will no more regard unconscious people discussing irrelevant topics

And you   man
Yes   you!
You'd rather change your optics now   Move
and carry on!

Amenity is a trap.

BEING GOLDFISH
SEEMS EASY
UNTIL
YOU ARE.

HOW TO TAKE CARE OF A GOLDFISH

Fresh air
Fresh water
Fresh mood everyday

Being goldfish means being able to forget anything bitter or joyous
In two minutes

The advantage of being goldfish is having a big world in a small space

Being goldfish is to be kind to all living things

To be joyful
To be accepting

Being goldfish is
to swim fast and faster everyday to build a *mémoire*
to swim fast and faster everyday and not going anywhere

Peer out and stare through the glass panes

Pointless odysseys
with few spontaneous stimulations

Being goldfish is to be transparent Here but not here
There but not there
All physical realms
are illusions.

How to take care of a goldfish then?

You must be free of shivers
angst
woe
and obsession

How to take care of a goldfish?

You must be free of confidence
melancholy
and satisfaction

To take care of a goldfish
is to accept aeons

Doom Boom

Wheel of fortune

Karma turns Karma Turns.

THE ORIGIN

She left her last bit of baggage
in Bucharest
where her nice blue jumpsuit had been robbed
at the final bachelor party. O vodka, ahah, guerilla!

She left
her forty square-metre studio
her cactus babies, her poetry books

the smell of cocktails and cherry lipstick
the smell of coconut handcream—she left her smell
diffused around the town
then disappeared in two seconds.

Her favourite blue windows
face Târgoviste.
Silhouette of yesterday afternoon.

She travels and lives like an amphibian.
Jump and burp. Jump and burp.
Voyage entre la terre et mer.
Carpe diem pour de vrai!

She has a green passport and lots of white shorts,
falling in love like a teen
grieving like an old, dark, oak tree
from Madeira to Madagascar. Bali to Mali.
India to Herzegovina.
A vagabond who drinks *mini*, *caffè coretto*, and *awamori*.

But last night she had a nightmare.

She had left her eagerness in a GAP country, she was blocked by a big man in uniform because of the satin on her head. The man said that she was not allowed to (fart in the airport or) wear satin on her head.

« "Do as I say: no satin on the head. Throw it away! » he said
« I don't see what I've done wrong here, sir » she replied
« The human race is costly: like burgers, like gods » he reasoned
« So just let me go home then... Send me home! » she dared him
« We are still following procedure here! Where have you come from, where do you want to go? » he asked
« I don't know. Everywhere. My home is everywhere. You can take me everywhere. I don't care…» and she began to cry.

They were tears of defeat, because of being denied being everywhere.
Her tears became a river.

She is awakened by the cold.

Witnessing her face with satin on her head, she makes new plans:
till her next itinerary
till her next foray. Till her next guise and disguise.

In the name of the origin
she flies.

I ASKED THE WORLD AND THE WORLD ASKED BACK

I still have not received any answers yet.
But I know something about the connections.

Like when a new coffee shop in my *quartier* seems like
the place I knew before I was born.

Like when I just knew
which flower's petals drooped for the first time this morning.

A beautiful lady's smile gave me her twenty-two suggestions for surviving adult life in one blink of an eye. I believe she could smell my fear. My fear for every second that will happen in the future.

And when I get trapped in these situations, usually I smile back.
Mind versus mind, *right?*
Well, an eye for an eye.

I am okay.
I hope you are okay too.

In this fragile world
we are all the same.
Feeling sorry and desperate about war
but easily getting bored of nature and its gifts.

We want more.
We always want more. And many.

Prediction and hypothesis. Contradictions everywhere.

We choose the places we go like we choose the kind of life we want.
I have chosen a grocery shop as my preferred destination.

There I can see the eyes of many fishes. Till I get lost in the battle.

Hell, I know nothing about everything.

LIPSTICK STAINS

TO ALL THE MOTHERS IN RED DRESSES AND BRAVERY.

Lipstick stains are everywhere
in my home

Wine glasses
Mirror in the bathroom Forehead of son
Diaper of baby
Shirt of husband
White cover of a book

Red for statement, not solely for existence
Red for braveness, to conquer the day

Like all mothers of my mothers Lipstick stains are a symbol
of beauty and sadness
passion and craziness

A balance
Substance imaginary
and logical daily routines.

TO OUR WHITE HUSBANDS

'I LOVE YOU. I LOVE YOUR SPECTRUM, IMPARTIALITY AND AWARENESS.'

That night we were melting in a fire
a fire of fondness and intelligence
an intelligence of ardour
an ardour of armour
an armour is our love kept in liberty
a liberty to call a human a human
not human as a label
not a label of *patriarcado*
No patriarcado del padre de los pecadores.
Lo tengo,
te amo.
Y nuestros hijos son grises.

TO THE BROKEN SISTERS OVER THERE
PLEASE USE MY HEART AND EVERYTHING I HAVE
TO HEAL YOU NOW.

PROJECT V

I enter the white cave filled with white roses and white candles. I think I am alone, lost in this cave of madness. I continue to walk to the vulva space. *A space of pleasure*, says the whispering voice (I don't know where it comes from). *Look for the crown.* I step forward, I turn to the left, then turn to the right, I jump three times and bow my head. I look around and see my shadow shaped in pink. So beautiful. The sunlight here is also pink. Breaks into the mighty flowers. Smells of roses. Wait for a minute. I hear a woman's scream. I think she is hurt. I run. Run. Run to the source of the voice. And I see. I see the spark. I can't believe my eyes. But I feel joy and amusement. Women in white dresses are spinning around, riding a carousel. They look happy. They are groaning from orgasm. Their bodies move here and there sensually, one of the women with her gorgeous magenta skin and black hair lets go of the carousel handle and she yells with happiness. I can smell the perfume of organa I know so well. Above the carousel there is a sign saying 'LABIOS MENORES'. One woman with her very cute rounded belly asks me to join the carousel. I wake up from my trance and ride a horse. GEEEEEEEEEEEEEEEEEEE!!! I feel vibrations everywhere. My ears, my leg, my chest are getting so warm, so warm, so hot. My soul is vibrant.

No man in the world can give me this satisfaction. I scream. I scream with joy and celebrate womankind. After half a day of riding the carousel we eat meat and apples. Then we sleep together amongst the leaves and flowers. When I wake up later I will be anonymous. I'll sign the white paper filled with laws and send you to prison. My head still hurts from the flying chair you hit me with last night. I was hurt. But it's over now. I hug my knees. Take a deep breath and sleep on my very own freedom.

THE GOLD LETTER

Nope. I never imagined this would happen in my lifetime. Like a breeze on a dry day. My hands are opening your white envelope now. I am studying this precious object carefully. It's not really white, I mean not white white. The envelope is milky white, so creamy, so elegant. Like you. Not *blanche neige* nor white rabbit. Not a virgin white either. You've chosen some goldfish sketches to add some energy. Or just to cheer up the recipient. These goldfish are very energetic indeed. They remind me of you crying and screaming at night. Funny. They don't remind me of goldfish inside small aquariums. They're so red and so merry, like a dream of a never-ending love story. You are living life in your own vivacity, in your own way. Your new adventures will not include my reality. Don't worry. I know where the line is. Oh… buoyancy! I thought the type would be in gold ink, but nope. It's red. Like a statement. A statement of femininity. A statement to tell everyone that we can be happy and angry at the same time. My dear, you have chosen your life's laughter. I hope your daily life will be lighter. The redness reminds me of lipstick. Women's weapon. You know, my dear. I can still remember your tiny hands touching my chest. And the blood in my veins getting hot. Burning with love. I am sure, I am, I will come to your wedding next week, my daughter. My lantern in a glass tube. You chose to be happy, you are always happy. By fluke, then swim! you little Seine. But don't forget to breathe. And do remember your redness everytime the water is not so pure.

HORN

Egypt has the right level of heat for my passions of the flesh. The pink one, the flesh with so many muscles. The smell of *masculinos papados amoroso.* And hrr hrr hrr hrr! Then goodbye in the morning. I only see the sun rise with someone I love and don't have. I don't have anyone. The acceptable morning news on the smart TV channel will be ready to hit the public at seven in the morning when I am not still not up. Still in bed with my two legs in the air. And *c'est la vie*, you can't solve problems with your vanilla-flavour electronic cigarette. Nor with your lotus position. Fighter fights, lover loves; let the horn get burnt. On the vintage blue glass vase I vomited twice after the erection in the belly and the hurry-up afternoon sex. Mr Brownie is ready to be humble while his wife gets ready to rumble. With extra words and the almost-naked summer pictures, we spell:

Life
Horn
Life
Horn's life
Rhyme
Lyric
Well-known poets

Sunflare is what I need now
Hymn
Basic
Humans and their highbrow habits
Supernova is what I need now
Horn is the logical subject of any physical form
Adjust your admiration of bodies. And one two three—
for the very first time I want to be
a number.

SYNTHESIS

Your institution, Sir, will be in recipience of my bunch of innovations.
Power, addiction, adoration
in a permanent exhibition.
Sir, this is where we had to demand joy and relief
with brave hearts and belief.
Children are the eyes of life and the adults are full of psychological baggage.
We are stuck conforming to this alien life in the name of cables.
Infrastructure, Sir, informs how I declare my world-class statements.
I am not green, Sir, I am a genius baby boy born of an angel.
I am ready to work by your side, Sir: in your western West I took your label.
And let me start to speak, Sir, about the politics of the new ages.
My grandmother told me to hang above life and smile at strangers.
And me and me and me, Sir, let me forget my skin, my mother language, Sir,
my mother, my oily land, my president, my brother, my life, Sir.
Let me forget my life and let me go inside your capital, Sir,
your generous capitaaaaaaaaaal.

CI LUK BA

Ci luk ba! Ci luk ba! Ci luk ba! Today is a happy day because Marni is in her home country with Adora and Madeira, her children of love. They are laughing and singing together, they're holding hands in trust and true honour. People are staring at their completely different appearances, watching them for entertainment. They respond to them with a smile. They use three languages to say the scenery is so beautiful. They take flowers and put them on their heads. A white man is standing nearby and taking beautiful pictures of them. He also yells at them about his love, legacy and divergence. Again, they respond to him with a smile. The white man says *Ci luk ba!* and they reply with *Ci luk baaa!*

AT NOON

It was noon. A jet plane discovered the sky. White marks and a blue background. I have been talking to myself about what will happen in the next nine months. Questioning life, domiciled.

Womanised. Shaping the points of construction. House, homicised. I see my goldfish doesn't move anymore in the fishbowl. I take it in my bare hands, put in the toilet, flush it away.

HIGHBALL

People love to watch a tragedy. People love other people to disappear. They love to see the pain. They love to see the torture. It's been eleven hours now since we put our trust in that famous search engine. When will the cyclone be near. At what time should we pray together and call our families. Oh no! Oh no! It's coming! The wind is blowing. And I am panicking, looking for whiskey to make a very Japanese highball. After my three glasses, I have a staring battle with my super ugly goldfish. *Abunai yo! Abunai yo! Abunai yo!*

ABOUT THE EMMA PRESS

The Emma Press is a small, independent publisher dedicated to producing beautiful, thought-provoking books for adults and children, with a special focus on poetry. It was founded in Winnersh in 2012, by Emma Wright, and is now based in the Jewellery Quarter in Birmingham. The Emma Press has been shortlisted for the Michael Marks Award for Poetry Pamphlet Publishers in 2014, 2015, 2016 and 2017, winning in 2016.

Visit the Emma Press website: theemmapress.com

CONTENTS

The Goldfish 1
To The Gentle River 5
Rebellion Red 7
How To Take Care Of A Goldfish 10
The Origin 12
I Asked The World And The World Asked Back 16
Lipstick Stains 18
To Our White Husbands 19
Project V 21
The Gold Letter 23
Horn 24
Synthesis 26
Ci Luk Ba 28
At Noon 29
Highball 30